## The Horizon of Possibility

Stars in a toolbox, shiny and bright,
Galaxies tangled, oh what a sight!
Planets in piles, just trying to fit,
Asteroids rolling, they just won't sit.

Cosmic blueprints flapping in space,
Builders in pajamas, what a disgrace!
Nebulae giggling, paint splattered wide,
While comets are arguing, 'Not my side!'

Original title:
Universe Under Construction

Copyright © 2025 Creative Arts Management OÜ
All rights reserved.

Author: Kieran Blackwood
ISBN HARDBACK: 978-1-80567-841-0
ISBN PAPERBACK: 978-1-80567-962-2

## Whispers of Galactic Craft

Listen closely, the cosmos is buzzing,
'Who put that star there?' the aliens are fussing.
With hammers and wrenches, young creatures delight,
Building a black hole, oh what a fright!

Mars is requesting new craters for fun,
While Jupiter's hoping for more moons to run.
Everyone's laughing, from Vega to Zed,
While Pluto just wonders, 'Where's my thread?'

## **Cosmic Layouts**

Templates of stardust, scattered around,
Cosmic designs with giggles abound.
Earth's on lunch break, sipping on tea,
While Saturn's rings dance—look, one for me!

Uranus just grumbled, 'Not that way, please!'
As meteors whizzed by with elegant ease.
Smaller moons snickered, filled with ambition,
Cosmic creativity, what a condition!

## Reimagining Celestial Constructs

Sketching up novas with crayons of light,
Doodles of planets, oh what a sight!
Supernovae giggle, with blasts of delight,
While black holes chuckle, 'We'll pull you in tight!'

Constellations arguing, 'You're upside-down!'
While stardust confetti falls all around.
Crafting the heavens, a messy affair,
Yet in the void, there's nothing to wear!

## **Beyond the Cosmic Veil**

In a workshop beyond the stars,
Galactic builders fix their cars.
With Lego blocks of bright design,
They craft each planet, oh so fine.

Asteroids are the missing parts,
While comets play their flashier charts.
Black holes serve as coffee pots,
While aliens knit with cosmic knots.

### Celestial Future

Planets spin on a cosmic line,
With traffic jams of stars that shine.
They honk and beep with laughter bright,
Chasing dreams through the endless night.

Nebulae in vibrant hues,
Brush cosmic dust on their shoes.
They joke and laugh, all in a swirl,
Like children playing in a whirl.

## Unfinished Realities

Time ticks by on a rattling clock,
While space monkeys fix the cosmic block.
Each galaxy's a puzzle, half-solved,
With funny quirks they've all evolved.

Gravity takes a coffee break,
While dancers float and giggle and quake.
They spin through loops, a silly dance,
In this realm of chance and circumstance.

## Mapping the Unknown

A map so vast, it makes no sense,
Yet cosmos scribblers take the defense.
They scratch their heads, count stars in twos,
And restyle orbits in mismatched shoes.

With crayons made of stardust bright,
They doodle planets late at night.
Drawing blobs that wobble here and there,
It's a cosmic mess, but who does care?

## Starlight Under Repair

Twinkling bulbs in cosmic space,
They're flickering, what a silly race!
With wrenches and glue, they tackle the dark,
While comets pass by with a honking lark.

Planets in line for a fresh coat of paint,
Jupiter's giggles, while Saturn can't faint!
A star up on stilts, just trying to shine,
Yelling to the moon, 'Hey! It's your time to dine!'

Asteroids bouncing like they're on a spree,
Space is a workshop, as zany as can be!
With hammers a-thudding and rockets that pop,
It's a cosmic carnival, never a stop!

## The Space We Build

Gather the stardust, let's get this done,
We'll craft a new planet, just for fun!
Spinning in circles, with glimmers and spark,
As meteors giggle and leave their mark.

Time for a dance in this brave new sphere,
Jiving with black holes, no need for fear!
Galaxies swirl like they're on a spree,
Building new orbits by the cup of tea.

Rockets are singing with paintbrush in hand,
Constructing a playground, oh isn't it grand?
With cosmic confetti and comets on skates,
Our joyful construction never hesitates!

## Cosmic Schematics

Grab a pen, let's sketch on the sky,
A plan for the stars that's wobbly and spry!
We'll draft a few planets, a moon with a smile,
Galaxies swirling in a twinkly file.

Doodles of comets with pink polka dots,
Asteroids high-fiving in their silly spots!
A blueprint of fun, where laughter ignites,
Construction's a game, with no silly fights.

In this cosmic office, we sip on space tea,
While aliens giggle, oh can't you see?
Our cosmic schematics, a hilarious sight,
A merry adventure, through day and night!

## Framing the Firmament

We're measuring starlight, just a tad too bright,
Framing the firmament with all our might!
With a tick-tock here and a giggle there,
Building a skyline of wonder and flair.

Nailing down meteors with cosmic glue,
It's sticking, it's sticking, who knew it would do?
A humorous tableau, with quarks and quirks,
As gravity chuckles and gently lurks.

The sky's our canvas, let's paint it with glee,
With whimsical wonders for all to see!
So come grab a hammer, let's all join the spree,
In this playful firmament, wild and free!

## Workshop of the Heavens

Sparkling stars in a toolbox bright,
Cosmic hammers ready to smite.
Nebulas swirling, colors so bold,
Creating stories yet to be told.

Planets roll off the assembly line,
Some are clumsy, others just fine.
Asteroids chuckle as they fly by,
Wanting a gig as a comet in the sky!

These space workers wear helmets with flair,
Galactic laughter fills the air.
While black holes argue who's really they,
Rifts in the fabric just a silly play!

So grab your tools and join the fun,
Building wonders 'til day is done.
In the cosmic shop, with joy we sing,
Crafting the weirdest of everything!

## Galaxies In Flux

Spinning whims like pizza dough,
Galaxies trip and sway to and fro.
Twinkling lights in a dance so absurd,
Astrophysical pranks often occurred!

The Milky Way giggles with every swirl,
While Jupiter polishes its big, round pearl.
Even the cosmos cracks silly jokes,
While black holes play hide and seek with the folks!

A quasar dazzles, puts on a show,
With sparkles and flashes like a disco!
Through gravity's pull, the stars just glide,
In this cosmic carnival, let's take a ride!

So give a cheer as the comets zip,
In this grand bash, you won't want to skip.
Galaxies laugh, all in a jam,
Creating a waltz that goes blam, blam, blam!

## Dreams Shaping the Cosmos

Crafting wonders with cosmic clay,
Silly shapes that bounce and sway.
A planet shaped like a giant shoe,
Stomping the stars as it wanders through!

Time-forgetters in a playful spree,
Twirling through dimensions, wild and free.
Each crazy thought becomes a star,
Creating chaos – it's never too far!

Supernovae pop like confetti bright,
While clouds of gas throw a dazzling light.
In this playground where dreams come alive,
Tickling time in a cosmic jive!

So join the fun, let your mind expand,
From floating thoughts to a starry band.
In the light of laughter, the cosmos gleams,
Shaping the night with our silliest dreams!

## Reflections of a Growing Expanse

In the mirror of space, what do we see?
A galaxy grinning, full of glee.
Stars taking selfies, oh, what a sight,
Bubbles of laughter that light up the night!

The night sky's an artist with colors to spare,
Painting the void with a whimsical flair.
Comets giggle as they streak on by,
Drawing funny faces across the sky!

With every twinkle, a jest in the air,
As planets jostle, never a care.
While meteors race in a playful dash,
Making wishes in sparkles, all happening fast!

In this vast canvas where joy takes flight,
The great expanse giggles, a pure delight.
So join the dance in this cosmic prance,
For every star sparkles in a lively romance!

## Astral Foundations

In the cosmos, builders toil,
With pencils made of silver foil.
They draw the stars with quirky flair,
A blueprint taped to cosmic air.

Galaxies spin like plates on stands,
With every twist, they drop their plans.
Black holes sigh, 'Oh what a mess!'
While comets sport a new address.

Wormholes fold like paper cranes,
While aliens play in cosmic lanes.
Construction hats with glitter and shine,
As they snack on asteroids, oh so fine!

A rocket's got a brand new coat,
With candy stripes and a goat to float.
As stars take turns to dance and jig,
The cosmos laughs at each new gig.

## The Milky Way's Makeover

In the Milky Way, a spa day found,
With twinkling stars all gathered round.
Each nebula gets a polish bright,
While black holes debate the latest flight.

They sprinkle stardust in the air,
While supernovae change their hair.
Planets choose their colors bold,
Painting rings of silver and gold.

Meteor showers shine their bling,
As space squirrels begin to sing.
With every galaxy's twirl and flip,
They giggle hard at the cosmic trip.

Through all the glitz and cosmic cheer,
The stars unite, 'Let's all draw near!'
To throw a party, oh so grand,
And dance across the stellar land.

## **Planets in the Workshop**

In a workshop where the stardust flows,
Planets toil, each with their woes.
Mars is stuck with a rusty paint,
While Venus screams, 'I need a saint!'

Saturn's rings in tangled knots,
Jupiter offers some intense thoughts.
'Hold my wrench,' Neptune shouts loud,
As Pluto's huddled, feeling proud.

With meteor tools and cosmic glue,
They fix each crater, paint it anew.
Asteroids roll by for a laugh,
As they measure space with an old giraffe.

When lunchtime strikes, they munch on light,
Biting at stars with pure delight.
In this celestial place of fun,
The workshop hums until they're done.

## Constellations in Creation

Constellations dot the sky with glee,
As they sketch their shapes, happy as can be.
Orion trips on his own long bow,
While Ursa Major steals the show.

With crayons bright, they doodle fast,
Creating legends that are meant to last.
Shooting stars get caught in the fun,
As they race each other, one by one.

The Big Dipper spills its drink,
While Cassiopeia winks and blinks.
They giggle at their silly forms,
As cosmic laughter takes new norms.

In the night, the tales unfold,
Of mischief hidden, legends bold.
In a galaxy where joy's a constant wave,
The constellations dance and rave.

## The Blueprint of the Infinite

In a workshop of stars and spark,
The architect scribbles, leaving his mark.
With a wrench and a screw, he'll build a new moon,
While humming a tune to a cosmic cartoon.

Galaxies swirling in paint so bright,
He miscounted planets, what a sight!
One got a crater, the other a groove,
As comets dance by in a stellar move.

With hammers of light, they shape and they mold,
Jokes about asteroids, they never get old.
The blueprints are funny, a few lines off,
Yet laughter erupts as the quarks scoff.

As cosmic dust settles into a pile,
They step back together, it's quite a style.
"Who knew building worlds could be such a blast?"
They've signed their creation, a smile cast.

## **Cradling the Astral**

A baby star's crying, it needs a good hug,
While planets spin gently, snug as a bug.
Astronauts wave, wearing diapers so grand,
Tossing stardust like it's glitter from hand.

In a nursery orbit, they rock and they roll,
Singing lullabies in a black hole bowl.
Galactic mobiles wobble and sway,
As toddlers of time giggle, laughing away.

The moons play peek-a-boo in cosmic delight,
While comets jump out with a spark and a flight.
"Oh look, there's Saturn in a cute little dress!"
Astral cradles giggle, embracing the mess.

With a rattle of quarks, the little ones sleep,
Guarding their dreams in stellar deep.
With crayons of light, they draw and they dream,
Crafting a cosmos that bursts at the seam.

## Fractured Light and Space

A photon tripped over a curvy old line,
"Hey, watch where you're going!" exclaimed old time.
Gravity chuckled, letting out a grin,
While space-time hiccuped, "Let the fun begin!"

Black holes are having a cosmic parade,
Sucking up all of the light in the shade.
Spaghetti and meatballs, that's quite the mess,
As stars take a tumble, but they still feel blessed.

The fabric is snagged, a cosmic enchant,
With quasars and quasars, they all do a dance.
Photons tumble, like ducks in a row,
"Oops, there goes a galaxy! Whoa, look at it glow!"

So twisty and turny, a playful retreat,
Each twist of the light finds a new way to meet.
In laughter that echoes through dark and through bright,
We play with the chaos, fracturing light.

## The Architecture of Dreams

In dreams made of stardust, architects play,
Sketching new worlds, in a whimsical way.
With blueprints of wishes and galaxies wide,
They draft up adventures where comets can ride.

Brick by brick, they build a grand gate,
For wandering thoughts, oh isn't it fate?
With windows of wishes and doors all ajar,
They invite floating thoughts with a ride on a star.

Bubbles of laughter, they whirl through the night,
Chasing down echoes, to share in delight.
With a sprinkle of starlight, they raise up their dreams,
While giggles grow louder, or so it seems.

In the morning they sigh, with a wink and a grin,
For the architecture of dreams lives forever within.
A canvas unfinished, oh let's make it gleam,
With giggles and stardust, let's build a new dream.

## The Constellation Codex

Stars are just dots on my cheat sheet,
I scribble them down, trying to compete.
Mars is just stuck in an awkward pose,
Wonder how long till it strikes a rose.

Planets in line, they wait for their cue,
But one rolls away, as if it knew.
"Hey, bring that back!" I shout with a grin,
But it just waves back, and dives right in!

My telescope's broken, it's off on a quest,
Caught an asteroid, it's found a new fest.
Each night's a party, with comets as guests,
I'm just a bouncer doing my best.

Galaxies swirl in a curious dance,
Stardust sprinkled on chance after chance.
I'll chart out the chaos with crayons in hand,
Creating a map for this wild little land!

## Cartography of the Unseen

With paper and pencil, I sketch out the void,
Finding new places, oh joy can't be avoid!
A black hole's a pit stop, where socks go astray,
Let's mark it with pencils, then run far away!

Nebulas loop like spaghetti on my page,
I'll add meatballs later, wait, that's all the rage!
The stars have refused to sit still for long,
But I'll sing them a tune, and hope they sing along.

Drawn maps and doodles fill my craft store,
Each galaxy's a gift, I just can't ignore.
Aliens giggle at my silly designs,
"Where's your compass?" they ask, "A little more lines!"

I'll label the bumps and the cosmic debris,
With arrows and hearts, for all to see.
Who knows what we'll find in this artful mischief?
I'll be the captain, let's shift into rift!

## Infinite Blueprints

Laying blueprints for things that don't exist,
Drawing up plans that get lost in the mist.
A doubt comes knocking, "Are you sure this works?"
I chuckle and say, "Just add more quirks!"

Each star's a project, needs stickers and flair,
I've lost half of 'em somewhere in thin air.
Building a comet, I need sparkly glue,
For crafting a tail, that's just what I do!

Wormholes are tricky, they twist and they turn,
Falling through one, I'm bound to unlearn.
But oh what a ride, I'm not one to frown,
When rockets can double as merry-go-rounds!

In cells of my notebook, the chaos can thrive,
With doodles of planets, the mad can survive.
Crafting a cosmos where silliness reigns,
Dive into nonsense, and forget all the pains!

### Celestial DIY

Grab your tools, it's time for some fun,
Let's build a new moon, but just one!
Last time we tried, it bounced off the wall,
Now we need helmets, we're having a ball!

Planets in paint mixed with glitter and glee,
I'm a cosmic chef, come bake with me!
Stretch out the sun, just give it a twist,
Oops! There it goes, too bright to resist.

Black holes in boxes, they're all stocked for sale,
One taste of their contents, you're off on a trail.
Building a star isn't tricky at all,
Just remember not to let it drop or fall!

As meteors fly by in a clumsy ballet,
We'll laugh and we'll giggle, come join in the play.
With cosmic repairs and some fairy dust spritz,
We're crafting the heavens, our laughter won't quit!

## **Loom of Stardust**

In a cosmic workshop, stars are stitched,
Galaxies tangled, a mix that's bewitched.
Planets roll in like marbles on the floor,
While comets whip by, yelling, "Look, there's more!"

Aliens giggle at the cosmic mess,
Building black holes, with a touch of finesse.
They sip on stardust, and laugh till they cry,
Over the screw-up where Earth got a pie.

Asteroids fall over, tripping on beams,
While cosmic cats chase interstellar dreams.
A nebula chuckles, puffing out its plume,
As space dust settles, creating new room.

Watch as the cosmos does its dance and spin,
With each silly mishap, it's a riotous din.
In this hilarious light, we all play a part,
Crafting the night with a giggle and heart.

## Pilgrimage to Creation

Wanderers of the void, with maps made of light,
Searching for answers, but losing their sight.
With floppy space boots that squeak with each tread,
They trip over planets and joke while ahead.

"What's that shiny thing? A star or a pie?"
They pull on their telescopes, squint at the sky.
A comet rolls by, dressed in sparkly wear,
"Is that a new fashion? Oh, do I dare?"

Black holes are like vacuum dads on a spree,
Swallowing dust bunnies, oh, what can't they see?
They mumble and grumble, but it's all in good fun,
As they tussle with quarks till the day is all done.

So join in the laughter, let joy take its flight,
As we pilgrimage further, chasing after the light.
With giggles and grins, we'll create all anew,
In a patchwork of chaos, there's room for the crew.

## Artifacts of the Beyond

What's that shiny object? An artifact bright,
Left by strange beings who jumped into night.
A chair made of starlight, a sofa of dust,
Wouldn't you try it? It's totally a must!

A sign in the cosmos, "Beware of the quarks,"
Humor in particles, making their marks.
Silly inventions from places unknown,
A toaster for comets, it's truly well-grown.

The laughter of quasars rings out in the dark,
As they juggle with electrons, and tease with a spark.
A calendar made of the universe's posts,
Proclaims all the holidays, from aliens' boasts.

So sift through the treasures, find gags in each nook,
As we celebrate chaos in this cosmic book.
With each shiny artifact, new laughter to find,
In the quirky collections, they've left us behind.

## Charting the Celestial Seas

Grab your star maps, it's time to set sail,
Through cosmic waters, we'll weave quite the tale.
Planets like jellybeans bob in the flow,
While swinging on comets, the star fishes glow.

Navigators chuckle, "Is that Jupiter's hat?"
As they push through the waves with a wink and a spat.
With telescopes for scoops, they gather up dreams,
Baking up theories like frothy whipped creams.

"Land ho!" cries a friend, as they spot a new star,
That's spinning around like a merry-go-car.
A sea of bright stardust, they navigate free,
With laughter and joy, charting blissfully.

# Hidden Designs of Matter

In a lab down the street, they're mixing up dreams,
With beakers and bubbles and wacky machine schemes.
Particles dance in giggles, swirling with glee,
As scientists ponder 'What could this be?'

Quarks in tight tutus, twirling around,
Making up rules they barely have found.
They chortle and chuckle, devising new tricks,
Creating a cosmos of odd little clicks.

Each atom's a rebel, it won't play it straight,
They're bending the laws—just testing their fate.
Add a wink from a neutron, a shimmy from gas,
And suddenly, voila! A strange-looking mass!

The fabric of space gets all tangled in yarn,
With colorful doodles that look like a farce.
Yet somehow it sparkles, as if it believes,
That chaos can fashion the worlds that it weaves.

## **Vistas Under Construction**

The stars are on break, while the comets repair,
With hammers and nails, they're fixing the flare.
A moon with a wrench is tightening bolts,
Retouching the craters for more lovely jolts.

Black holes are digging, making new space,
Looking for places to hide their disgrace.
Those twinkling lights say, 'Hang tight, we'll glow!',
As they paint on new dreams with interstellar flow.

Galaxies shift, like a yard sale in flight,
Swapping their colors, all flashy and bright.
The cosmic architect sipping on stars,
Sighs at the traffic from Jupiter's cars.

Oh, what a sight! It's a riot up there,
With aliens laughing, not a single care.
They're building a playground, a park in the sky,
Where nebulae giggle and planets all fly!

## Breathing Space into Reality

A thought floated by, let's give it some air,
With balloons of imagination, we'll go anywhere!
Bubbles of joy drift, each filled up with cheer,
Turning wishes to stars that shimmer so near.

A rocket's in line for a cosmic repair,
With duct tape and dreams, it's floating in flair.
They're checking the gauges, adorned with a grin,
And laughing at how they fit all of them in.

The comets are coaching, 'Just blast off with flair!',
While meteors cheer from the interstellar fair.
Clouds of confetti and sparkles converge,
As everyone joins in the wild cosmic surge.

Reality bends under giggles and light,
As everyone huddles for structure and spite.
Painting the starry scene vibrant and wild,
With dreams as the canvas, by laughter compiled!

## Whispered Blueprints of Fate

When plans get scribbled on cosmic blue sheets,
The universe chuckles with mischievous beats.
Plans for a supernova sprout lively designs,
But destiny playfully twirls all the lines.

The suns hold debates, with bright ideas glowed,
While planets plot pranks on the paths they once strode.
A comet slips in, with a wink and a grin,
As chaos brings laughter, 'Let's do it again!'

The builders of fate are all thumbs and all toes,
Stirring up mischief where no one quite knows.
With giggles and snickers, they draft out their schemes,
While stars spin in circles, burst out with beams.

As fate tosses darts, wrapped in balloons,
The universe dances to whimsical tunes.
With snaps and a spark, the designs come alive,
In a world full of laughter, once more we arrive!

## The Sky's Canvas

The stars are not quite straight,
They're hanging by a thread.
Cosmic artists on a break,
With glitter on their head.

Planets spin in silly ways,
Like tops gone wild in flight.
Comets slip on banana peels,
And giggle through the night.

Black holes play hide and seek,
With asteroids that roam.
They're laughing in the dark,
While working from their home.

Jupiter's throwing a space bash,
With rings that twist and twirl.
Saturn's moons are on the floor,
Doing the cosmic whirl.

## Chasing Celestial Dreams

I chased a shooting star,
It laughed and zipped away.
It said, 'Catch me if you can!'
And danced in bright ballet.

The clouds were caught in giggles,
As I tripped on stardust trails.
Gravity forgot to pull me down,
As I flew with silly sails.

Asteroids were throwing pies,
At planets round and blue.
I ducked and dodged like crazy,
Oh, where's my superstar crew?

The moon's playing peekaboo,
Behind a fluffy veil.
You'd think it lost its glasses,
In this cosmic, fun-filled tale.

## Sketching the Night

With crayons made from starlight,
I draw constellations bright.
But every time I turn around,
They giggle and take flight.

Orion's trying to flex his arms,
But he's more like a string bean.
While Cassiopeia strikes a pose,
In a cosmic fashion scene.

The Milky Way spills its secrets,
Like an overstuffed piñata.
Candy bars fall from the sky,
In this sweet galactic saga.

I paint a rocket red,
Then watch it turn to blue.
It says, 'I'm off to find some fun,'
And vanishes from view.

## Echoes Among the Stars

I heard a starburst giggle,
As it bounced from here to there.
It said, 'We're all just playing,
In this vast and open air.'

Neptune's singing off-key tunes,
While comets clap along.
The echoes dance and swirl about,
In a cosmic, silly song.

Galaxies do the tango,
While black holes spin in glee.
They're waltzing in the dark,
As planets sip their tea.

Supernova's popped confetti,
Sprinkling joy on all sides.
In this chaotic cosmos,
Where every star abides.

## Foundations of the Unknown

The stars are hammering away,
Building dreams in broad daylight.
Galactic blueprints tossed about,
Space gets messy in the night.

A comet trips over a beam,
While Saturn wears a crooked hat.
Black holes giggle, 'Is it a dream?'
Could this be where we lost the cat?

Each planet's a work in progress,
With paint that drips and tools that squeak.
They argue over who's the best,
While galaxies whisper, 'Let's tweak!'

So if you gaze into the skies,
And see chaos, don't look away.
Know there's laughter with each surprise,
In this grand show, we're here to play.

## **Cosmic Hands at Work**

Jupiter's trousers are a sight,
Stitched up with moons, oh what a mess!
Mars is busy, fixing a light,
While stars dance in their work address.

Each black hole swallows a sandwich,
'Visit the sun, it's quite the trip!'
But watch for space's mischievous inch,
Where gravity makes you do a flip!

Comets whizz by with a giggle,
Building bridges made of dreams.
And meteors tease with a jiggle,
When cosmic chaos bursts at the seams.

So if you float through the night sky,
Grin at the cosmic pandemonium.
We're all part of this playful tie,
At the heart of a vast melodium.

# Fragments of Infinity

Pieces of stars scatter wide,
As spacetime plays a little game.
Asteroids bump and take a ride,
Yelling, 'We're just here for fame!'

The Andromeda hairdo's a mess,
Neptune's wearing mismatched socks.
While comets sport a trendy dress,
Collecting stardust in their docks.

Planets gossip, sharing their fears,
'What if we're all just a cartoon?'
While Saturn spins with cosmic cheers,
Singing 'We'll party till noon!'

So watch the night come to life,
With a wink and a twinkling star.
Amidst the cosmic joy and strife,
We're all just fragments, near and far.

## The Nebula's Blueprint

A nebula scribbles its plans,
With crayons and glitter (how neat!).
While a star looks on and just stands,
Hoping for a chance to compete.

Pulsars throw a wild party,
With lights that blink in varied hues.
It's a cosmic bash, so hearty,
But don't forget the space-time blues!

Constellations form a conga line,
Twirling around in stretch-shaped shoes.
While meteors shout, 'Look how we shine!'
As the universe spills jests and clues.

With sketches of chaos in the air,
And the Milky Way wearing a crown.
Just know there's laughter everywhere,
In this cosmic circus, up and down.

## Fabric of Imagination

In the attic of thought, a spider spins,
Threads of giggles, hides where the fun begins.
A patchwork of daydreams, bright colors collide,
The fabric of wackiness, where nonsense can slide.

Balloons that float with a purpose unknown,
Juggling with stardust, the stars have been blown.
Giant rubber ducks in a celestial race,
Laughing at planets, making silly face.

Laughter erupts from a comet-shaped pie,
Shooting across the sky with a glint in its eye.
Wobbling galaxies on a teeter-totter,
As giggles create, the cosmos grows hotter.

Plot twists in cosmos, a riddle to bend,
Jokes told by black holes, on jest they depend.
With each witty wink, new worlds take a spin,
The fun never ceases; let the chaos begin!

## Fragments of the Unseen

In pockets of space, where reality plays,
Lost socks and lost thoughts dance in a maze.
A wink from a star, a nod from the moon,
Jokes tucked in nebulae, laughter in tune.

Invisible ink spills on the fabric of time,
Each moment a punchline, a doodle in rhyme.
Bubble wrap planets, so pleasing to pop,
Tickling the void, as silence takes a hop.

Rocket ships piloted by fluffy-haired cats,
They sail through the cosmos in colorful hats.
Witty remarks from the comets and suns,
Echo through the ages, all jests come in tons.

Lost in reflections of giggles and glee,
Snickering asteroids like bees round the tree.
Peeking at dimensions where chaos is found,
In fragments of laughter, the unseen astounds.

## The Forge of Celestial Dreams

In a workshop of wonders, hammers clang loud,
Bending the starlight to make a bright cloud.
Welding with whimsy, sparks fly every way,
Inventing new holidays, just for a play.

Amongst molten meteors, marshmallow stars,
Creating new worlds with candy guitars.
Popcorn for planets and soda for sun,
Every sip and each bite makes dreaming more fun.

Blueprints of laughter, drawn all over the floor,
With nibs made of stardust, they craft evermore.
Jokes weave like constellations, a giggle parade,
As cosmic caboodles their charades are displayed.

The forge of delight, with joyful designs,
Empowers the dreamers, gives laughter their signs.
In the heart of the realm, where silliness beams,
Dancing in stardust, they conjure up dreams.

## Pathways of Creation

Each path that we wander, a trail full of cheer,
Made of marshmallow fluff, and giggles we hear.
The stars guide our steps, like paint on the ground,
Where colors of laughter blend round and round.

Sketching the cosmos with crayons of light,
Tickling the darkness, illuminating the night.
With each funny detour, we shuffle and sway,
Imagining art in a whimsical way.

Clouds made of candy, rivers of taffy,
Guiding our journey through things that are wacky.
The laughter of comets, like an echo, resounds,
In pathways of madness, where joy knows no bounds.

Building new bridges from silly to wise,
In the heart of adventure, where nonsense can rise.
At the end of the road, where fun never wanes,
Creation keeps dancing on giggly refrains.

## Beyond the Pillars of Creation

In a workshop high, stars spin my way,
The hammer clangs, as comets sway.
With chisel and dream, I carve the night,
Building suns that glow with glee and light.

Galactic glue and cosmic tape,
Crafted with care—a funny shape!
Watch out! That nebula might just sneeze,
Exploding stardust like cosmic confetti trees.

The black holes giggle, they swallow in jest,
While planets play hide and seek like the rest.
I trip on moonbeams, landing astray,
Inventing worlds in a most silly way.

So when you look up at the vast night sky,
Remember there's laughter as stars swirl by.
Beneath our feet is building galore,
Creating a playground where wonders soar!

## **Navigating Stark Horizons**

I set sail on a spaceship of cheese,
Navigating stars like a cosmic breeze.
With an alien map that's covered in chili,
Every new planet makes me laugh till I'm silly.

The outer rings dance, they're quite the sight,
Wrinkled like an old man, but shining bright.
Asteroids wobble, don't ask them to race,
For they trip over orbit like a clumsy pace.

Galaxies swirl like they're having a ball,
Spaghetti and meatballs in the cosmic hall.
I call it dinner, with forks made of rays,
Twirling the stars in a pasta-like haze.

So grab your snacks and join my parade,
As we navigate chaos in cosmic charade.
The fabric of space is a riotous quilt,
Stitched with giggles and dreams we built!

## Lettering Across the Cosmos

With crayons of starlight, I draw the night,
Sending messages with galaxies in sight.
Each comet I carve holds giggles so grand,
A note from the cosmos, written in sand.

I scribble on meteors, jump in delight,
Whispering secrets in the soft twilight.
"Dear Earthling," it starts, "Things are quite weird,
We're trading stardust and laughter, not feared!"

The quasar replies with a wink and a grin,
"Dear friend from afar, let the fun begin!"
The light-years shrink, they wrap 'round like lace,
In this writing game, we all share space.

So send me a postcard from your tiny nook,
I'll write back with stars and a cosmic hook.
Together we'll laugh as we draft our new fate,
Forever exchanging interstellar greats!

## Shaping the Night

In the workshop of dusk, where shadows play,
I mold the dim light in a fanciful way.
With a twist and a turn, I pattern the glow,
Creating a skyline that tips with a show.

The moon's a big lamp, turned on just for kicks,
Wobbling playfully, doing funny tricks.
Stars are the glitter that giggle and spark,
They twirl in the sky, making their mark.

Meteor showers rain down like confetti,
A celebration of chaos, all jolly and jetty.
I swing from the comets, so wild and free,
Painting the night with sheer jubilee.

So let's toast to the night with these dreams we invent,
A universe laughing, no matter where we went.
Cosmic giggles echo, filling the air,
In this playful expanse, there's love everywhere!

## Ascending Dimensions

In a place where stars wear hard hats,
Planets spin while joking with bats.
Galaxies stretching, a cosmic ballet,
Building new realms, day by day.

Quasars are hoarding spanners and beams,
Crafting their dreams with whimsical themes.
Comets whizz by, but don't take a chance,
In this grand project, we all do a dance.

Black holes are sighing, 'We need more light!'
While nearby, suns are burning bright.
With laughter and chaos, the space crew glows,
Constructing horizons no one yet knows.

So grab your tools, and let's make a scene,
In the infinite realms of the unforeseen.
With a giggle and a wink, let's raise a cheer,
As dimensions ascend, and fun is here!

## **Transiting Through Time**

Time travelers meeting, what a sight,
Dressed in pajamas, ready for flight.
With clashing eras and quirky styles,
They swap their gadgets, it's full of smiles.

Wizards and robots in friendly debate,
Over who can teleport faster—wait!
Pouring their secrets in tea cups of fate,
They giggle at history, isn't it great?

Past, present, future, all in a row,
Each adding details to the timeline's flow.
With hiccups and laughs, they just can't believe,
How time keeps tripping; oh, what a reprieve!

So let's hop on a comet, and zoom through the years,
With space-time giggles, we'll conquer all fears.
In this playful tangle of temporal fun,
Every tick-tock echoes—come join us, everyone!

## Cosmic Canvas in Touch

With brushes of stardust and colors so bright,
Celestial artists begin their delight.
Swirling with laughter, they paint the night sky,
While meteors giggle as they zoom by.

Planets dip toes in the rainbow paint,
Creating strange shapes that none can complain.
Moons chase each other in a cosmic race,
All amidst splatters of glitter and lace.

Nebulas joining in an artful affair,
Crafting new wonders, spreading joy in the air.
In this gallery vast, imagination runs free,
With each brush stroke, a new galaxy.

So grab your palettes, let's join the parade,
In this whimsical world, no plans need to be made.
As stars wink and twirl, we'll paint without care,
Our cosmic canvas shines bright, everywhere!

## **Celestial Innovations**

In a lab made of stardust, ideas abound,
Aliens tinkering with shapes all around.
Gadgets and gizmos, what a wild spree,
Creating odd contraptions—look, it's a spree!

Gravity hiccups with newly found charms,
As constellations dance with their twinkling arms.
Time machines serving cosmic hotdogs,
While comets spin frisbees with giggly hogs.

Using black holes as portals for fun,
Teleporting snacks, yeah, that's how it's done!
With a whoosh and a zap, watch the stars play,
In this realm of inventions, the sky's the limit today!

So come join the laughter, let's build and create,
In a thriving cosmos that just can't wait.
With smiles and surprises, we'll bring forth a burst,
As we innovate joy; the universe's first!

## When Galaxies Take Shape

Stars twinkle and giggle, oh what a sight,
Planets wiggle as they take to flight.
Dust bunnies tumble in cosmic dance,
While comets prance in a starry trance.

Asteroids argue, 'Who gets the best spot?'
While black holes whisper, 'You can't catch what you sought.'
With each swirl and twist, gravity's the trick,
As nebulae bloom, go on, take your pick!

## The Infinite Worksite

Blueprints scattered like leaves on the ground,
Cosmic laughter echoes, a funny sound.
Workers in space wear helmets of gold,
As they hammer on stars, so brightly bold.

Wrenches clatter, and beams they do bend,
Galactic tools never seem to end.
Time clocks ticking in a comical way,
'Is it lunch yet?' they ask every day!

## **Cosmic Engineers at Play**

With a cosmic joke, they build and collide,
Giggling asteroids take joy in the ride.
Twirling galaxies with a mischievous grin,
While stardust sparkles as mayhem begins.

Space shuttles zoom like bees in a hive,
Cosmic engineers keep the fun alive.
Mixing up planets, a wild buffet,
'How about bananas?' they cheerfully say!

## New Worlds Rising

From bubblegum clouds, new worlds appear,
Dancing on rainbows, they spread out cheer.
With laughter and whimsy, they rise and they shine,
Creating a playground where planets do dine.

Toaster-shaped moons pop up with a blast,
As comets scream by, flying way too fast.
In this colorful chaos, the fun just won't end,
With a wobbly dance, the cosmos they mend.

## Stars in Development

In the workshop of the night, they tinker,
Stars in pajamas, with bright winks,
They drop their hammers, pout and ponder,
Creating constellations that rarely sync.

One says, "Hey, I'm a little too bright!",
Another shouts, "Who painted me green?",
They giggle and jostle, throwing starlight,
As they dance like they're on a cosmic screen.

Asteroids rolling, giggling away,
A comet gets stuck in the Milky Way,
While planets are spinning a bit out of place,
Drafting a map for their next big race.

So watch for the flashes, the sparkles, the beams,
As celestial buddies chase moonlight dreams,
In this chaotic but joyful night,
Crafting a sky that's delightfully bright!

## Galactic Renovations

Once on a ladder, the Sun had a plan,
"Let's make this sky a sprawling fan!",
With paint and glitter, it splashed around,
Re-decorating the night's vast ground.

The moons were amazed, "Are you sure we need flair?",
"What's wrong with the darkness? It's comfy in there!",
But in rolled comets with brushes galore,
And they argued for sparkles, wanting more decor.

Planets bickering over color schemes bright,
While asteroids debated the shape of the light,
The Milky Way whispered, "Let's all be unique!",
As they remodelled the heavens, cheeky and cheek.

Now the sky's a masterpiece filled with glee,
With a disco-ball star, as wild as can be,
The cosmos chuckled, a playful sensation,
In this endless realm of star-studded creation.

## Cosmic Unfolding

One day the cosmos decided to stretch,
To unfurl its arms with an elaborate sketch,
Stars doing yoga, oh what a sight,
As they reach for the moon with all their might!

Galaxies twirled and practiced their spins,
While black holes giggled, and light began to thin,
"Out with the old, let's make room for more!",
Cried the nebulae, excited to explore.

In the midst of the chaos, a quasar sneezed,
Sending stardust flying, they were all quite pleased,
"A galaxy's charm is to be free and spry!",
They declared with a wink under the watchful sky.

So if you look up and see stars collide,
Just know they're unfolding, not trying to hide,
Embracing the dance, the cosmic ballet,
In laughter and light, they just love to play!

## Nebulas in Progress

In a corner of space, with color and flair,
Nebulas work with a colorful stare,
Fluffing their edges, with sparkles in tow,
Crafting new shapes that really do glow.

Some are quite shy, hiding their hues,
While others are bold in vibrant reds and blues,
They giggle and puff, letting colors burst,
With cosmic giggles, a creative thirst.

One whispers, "What if we try polka dots?",
While another insists "Stripes are the hot shots!",
They mix up the gases, spin around fast,
Creating new ideas that are sure to last.

So when you gaze up at a colorful sight,
Remember the fun of these hazy nights,
In a swirling, twirling lab, they play and make,
A masterpiece brewing in every mistake!

### **Night's Pending Design**

The stars are on a coffee break,
Galaxies are misaligned, oh what a mistake!
A comet's lost its tail today,
Crafting chaos in a cosmic ballet.

Planets spin on crooked axes,
While aliens draw on cosmic glasses.
Black holes are just fancy vacuums,
Sucking up our space room fumes!

Nebulae spill glittering paint,
The universe went wild, but it ain't quaint!
Asteroids roam like they own the place,
While stardust giggles, setting the pace.

With each misplaced star and errant quark,
The night laughs on, bright and stark.
So let's sip stardust, toast to the mess,
In this grand design, we're all blessed!

## Weaving Through the Void

In the void, we plot and weave,
Threads of light that twinkle and cleave.
A cosmic spider spins her web,
Trapping jokes, that's what she said!

Quasars hum a catchy tune,
While meteors dance, kicking up a boon.
Hiding socks from Saturn's rings,
Making laundry a cosmic fling!

Wormholes twist like tongue-tied vines,
With portals opening at odd times.
Grab your popcorn, it's quite a show,
As starlight giggles and don't let go!

The dark is silly, it's true and bright,
With every blink, it's pure delight.
So here we are, in this playful flood,
Woven through, in cosmic mud!

## The Forge of Existence

In a forge where stars are born,
Cosmic chefs toss chaos, and out come horns!
They stir with laughter, sprinkle some spice,
Cooking up wonders, oh so nice!

Metals melt, conform and bend,
Creating planets just around the bend.
But oops! A moon got burnt and well,
Now it rolls in circles, what a tale to tell!

With interstellar hammers that boom,
They shape the cosmos in a room.
Billions of giggles spark the steel,
In this grand forge, we can feel!

So grab your goggles, join the fun,
In the heat of existence, we all run!
We're all but bits in the cosmic bake,
A laugh, a swirl, in this grand remake!

## Stars Yet to Light

In a gallery of future sights,
Stars are snoozing, waiting for nights.
They've hit the snooze, they'll rise and shine,
When the alarm goes off, all will be fine!

Galaxies wait with a wink and nudge,
Peek-a-boo from dark, they won't budge!
They'll throw a party, oh what a sight,
When they decide it's time to ignite!

Gravity's doing the hula dance,
Pulling on planets, giving them a chance.
While space dust giggles and rolls on through,
It's a cosmic prank, we're all in the brew!

So hold your breath, it's quite all right,
The show's about to start, 'neath the moonlight.
With stars yet to light in this cosmic spree,
We find our joy in the mystery!

## Horizons Yet to Rise

In the night, stars wear hard hats,
Building dreams with cosmic chats.
Planets trip on comets' tails,
While space dust sings of epic fails.

Rockets dance in clumsy glee,
Wobbling like a drunken bee.
Galaxies play hopscotch afar,
Each one hoping to be a star.

Astronauts juggle with moon rocks,
Attempting to fix the ticking clocks.
A black hole laughs, 'You can't escape!'
While quarks trade pranks with a cosmic cape.

As we watch the universe bake,
A giant cake made from stardust flake.
Bake it high, and watch it rise,
With sprinkles made of shooting skies.

## **The Fabric of New Realities**

Weaving dreams with cosmic thread,
Stitching space on a needlebed.
Tiny atoms throw a fit,
While wormholes play a game of split.

Molecules knit with a silly grin,
Chasing each other round and round spin.
Time giggles, 'Can I have a break?'
While gravity tries to keep it all awake.

Black holes host a wild rave,
Inviting quasars, oh how they behave!
Gravity pulls, but they can't resist,
As they twirl on a blurring list.

In this quilt of endless might,
Every patch is sewn tight.
Who knew chaos could be so fun?
As reality dances, it has just begun!

## **Gravity's Blueprint**

Gravity sketches with a laugh,
Scribbling lines that make math baff.
Planets wobble on designed tracks,
Bouncers checking cosmic snacks.

Comets fetch drinks from stardust bars,
While meteorites sign autographs with stars.
Rocket blueprints swirl 'round and round,
In a galactic mess on the ground.

The sun tries to stay on the ball,
Wobbling, wondering if he'll fall.
Moons giggle and hold their breath,
While dreaming of space's funny death.

An architect's view from distant shore,
Plans on napkins, galore and more.
As laughter echoes through the vast skies,
The galaxy blinks, in cosmic surprise!

## Cosmic Cauldron

In a pot where starlight brews,
Mixing flavors, and cosmic hues.
A dash of dark matter, sprinkle of fate,
Stirring up chaos, oh isn't it great!

Galactic chefs toss in some light,
A few quirks to make it just right.
With a pinch of laughter, they taste the air,
'What's next?' they ask, with curious flair.

The recipe calls for a pinch of fun,
As nebulae orbit, oh what a run!
Chef comets giggle while they blow,
Seeing what magic the cauldron can show.

So let's ladle servings across the stars,
Sharing giggles from Venus to Mars.
With a wink and a nod to everything sin,
In this cosmic kitchen, let the fun begin!

## A Tapestry of Stars

Stars knitting daydreams, in the cosmic loom,
Counting hiccups of laughter, under the moon.
Galaxies spinning like tops, in a shiny dance,
Comets with silly hats, take a wild chance.

Wormholes with party hats, swirling like fun,
Black holes eating cake, like it's a race won.
Nebulas giggle softly, with colors so bright,
While planets play tag, chasing the light.

## Laying the Groundwork for Tomorrow

Foundations of stardust, all set with glee,
Building blocks of laughter, for you and me.
Galactic architects, with rulers and pens,
Sketching out tomorrow, where nonsense begins.

Space mice with tool belts, tightening beams,
Wrenching away worries, sewing up dreams.
Planets on roller skates, whirling about,
Singing construction songs, shout it out loud!

## The Celestial Cookbook

Mixing stardust with giggles, a recipe grand,
Sprinkling laughter like salt, across the land.
Galactic pies cooling, in the cosmic breeze,
Baking comets and muffins, sprinkled with cheese.

Stir the Milky Way gently, don't spill a drop,
Add a dash of moonlight, let the good times bop.
Taste testing the planets, oh what a feat,
Each bite is a journey, a whimsical treat!

## Celestial Constructs

Planets clad in paint, a colorful spree,
Building rocket-shaped houses, under a tree.
Shooting stars are handymen, fixing up lights,
While space junk is gathered for creative sights.

Laughter echoes through rings, like a cosmic song,
With asteroids dancing, joining along.
Crafting a playground on the comets so spry,
Where the jolly giants bounce, waving goodbye!

## The Celestial Workshop

In the workshop of stars, bright and bold,
An alien painter is mixing up gold.
He spills a bit blue, and oh what a sight,
Now Jupiter dresses in denim at night.

With hammers that clang, and pencils that sway,
They measure the comets, come join in their play.
A moon's got a deadline, it's late with a laugh,
As Saturn insists on its rings made of half.

A star-shaped cookie cutter cuts through the haze,
As planets audition for cosmic ballet.
Galaxies giggle, and black holes discuss,
Who's the next star to get lost in the fuss?

And so they all toil in glorious cheer,
Crafting a cosmos that feels somewhat queer.
With each little blink, a new joke will unfurl,
In the grand workshop of our funny old world.

## Echoes of Tomorrow

In the echoing depths of a time travel shop,
Past fads resurface, like '80s hip-hop.
Dinosaurs dance in their disco suits,
While aliens giggle in cosmic pursuits.

They're scheduling dates with future selves,
Whispers of wisdom from quantum shelves.
A T-Rex promises not to fall,
While robots are line-dancing, having a ball.

The hourglass spins with a wink and a twirl,
As dreams take shape in a glittery swirl.
Crafting tomorrows with joy and delight,
Starships showcase their best disco lights.

Echoes of laughter bounce back and forth,
A giggling portal shows value in worth.
Each tick of the clock is a chance to explore,
Tomorrow's shenanigans, who could ask for more?

## Building Boundless Realms

In a garden of galaxies, laughter grows bright,
With builders who bungle while working at night.
They mix up dimensions, oops, what a mess,
Now Mars wears a tutu—oh, what a dress!

They stack up the planets like children with blocks,
Shooting stars squeal with unorthodox shocks.
Each realm has a playground with swings made of light,
While quasars are playing hide-and-seek in the night.

Meteors race with a big bouncy ball,
While comets compete in a laughter-filled brawl.
Aliens wobble in helmets too tight,
Delivering giggles as galaxies ignite.

So come to the grounds of this nonsensical spree,
Where wonders are woven with cheeky glee.
Building new realms with a wink and a cheer,
In this quirky playground, there's fun to be near!

## Stellar Architecture

In the realm of bright stars, a builder declared,
"I'll design a new planet, a model that's rare!"
They drew up blueprints with crayon and glue,
But forgot to account for a zoo and a stew!

With marshmallow mountains and lakes made of jam,
They crafted a home for each critter and clam.
A sun made of candy, oh sweet as can be,
But it melted too quickly and drew quite a spree.

The architect laughed as the planets spun fast,
While asteroids joined them, they built up their cast.
In a galaxy thriving on quirky designs,
Where each star's a page in hilarious lines.

So here's to the builders, both silly and grand,
Creating a cosmos that's funky and planned.
With each little quirk, a new layout's in store,
In this stellar architecture, we all want more!

### Fractals of Infinity

In a workshop of stars, they hammer away,
Galaxies giggle at what they display.
Comets make coffee, all buzzing with cheer,
While black holes are grumpy, 'Don't pull me in here!'

Nebulas dance, they twirl and they spin,
Building a world with a cheeky grin.
Planets in line for the cosmic parade,
Saying, 'I want rings! Please, don't be afraid!'

Asteroids chatting, they've got tales to share,
'Once I was part of a cosmic affair!'
While shooting stars nap in a comfy plume,
'Oh, the things we create could light up your room!'

In this workshop of fun, every blip is a joy,
Stardust crafting a brand new toy.
With each little giggle, new wonders arise,
A playground of chaos under glittery skies.

## The Cosmic Tapestry

Threads of starlight, so wobbly and bright,
Sewing up cosmos from day into night.
Quasars skip by on a colorful loom,
While spacetime unravels in a cosmic room.

Knitting some planets with yarn made of gold,
As meteors whiz, with stories retold.
Gravity jumps in, trying to keep pace,
'Hang on, little worlds, you're losing your place!'

Colors explode, a radiant mess,
'Next stitch is a black hole, but can we digress?'
Galactic grandmas tell tales with a wink,
'Now, where's that old comet? I need it to blink!'

With laughter and glee, they craft and they play,
Creating new wonders, come join the array!
In a cosmic patchwork, all things intertwine,
A funny adventure, divine and benign!

## Embers of Creation

Sparks of life dance on cosmic flames,
Creating small worlds, with funny names.
Planets are sizzling, fresh out from the pot,
'How about 'Goofus?' I think it's a lot!'

In a furnace where laughter ignites the space,
Supernovas chuckle in a flash of grace.
The elements giggle, mixing up their brew,
'Add a pinch of chaos, just for the view!'

Flames flicker, and cosmos starts to glow,
A recipe handed down, ancient and slow.
With cosmic seasoning, they stir up delight,
Painting the heavens both day and night.

And as they create, a great cheer erupts,
'From these playful embers, the universe jumps!'
With winks and with nudges, stars begin to shine,
It's a fun-filled creation, a grand design!

## Sculpting Time and Space

With chisels of light, the sculptors at play,
Shaping dimensions in a whimsical way.
Time giggles softly as it curves and it bends,
'Oh, don't rush me now, I'm just making friends!'

Space is a sponge, soaking in the hues,
'Let's add some polka dots, I choose the blues!'
Rulers of laughter measure quarks with glee,
'Why not make this one as silly as me?'

Carving out comets, with artistry so bold,
'Maybe this one should sparkle with gold!'
As shadows of planets dance in the light,
Even black holes have jokes that feel just right.

In this gallery cosmic, they're all in a trance,
Sculpting a story, an eternal dance.
Creating the absurd in every weave and place,
Time and space chuckle in this funny embrace!

## Starlit Scaffolding

In the night sky, wrenches cling,
Stars giggle as the comets swing,
Galaxies with glitter and paint,
Building dreams where angels faint.

Cosmic builders in a dance,
Planets twirl, a clumsy prance,
Meteors drop like tools from high,
While Saturn's rings just laugh and sigh.

Nebulae wrapped in duct tape bright,
Pulsars twinkle, nearly on strike,
Laughter echoes through the void,
In this realm, all chaos employed.

A sign reads: 'Please excuse our mess',
Under stars, we will digress,
For each quasar has its charm,
And chaos keeps the cosmos warm.

## A Symphony of Creation

Twirling stars in cosmic tunes,
Brass and bassoons make mischief soon,
Each black hole plays a solo grand,
While asteroids with cymbals stand.

Pluto brings his tuba in,
While jovial Jupiter wears a grin,
Satellites dance, a waltz, off-key,
As galaxies sway, how funny they be.

Supernovae burst with laughter bright,
Cracking stars in the deep of night,
A cosmic band with no refrain,
Creating joy amidst the pain.

In this symphony of bizarre delight,
Cosmic jesters join the plight,
For each note makes creation sing,
A melody to which we cling.

## **Nebulous Designs**

Sketching clouds with a sparkling pen,
Stars are stars, but why not hens?
Planets shaped like rubber ducks,
In this sketchbook, we have no luck.

Floating ideas on cosmic waves,
Black holes turn into quirky caves,
Galactic dreams in whimsical hues,
Drawn by creatures with space-age shoes.

Nebulae giggle in pastel tones,
While stardust scatters hard-as-stones,
A blueprint of laughter, what a sight,
In this cosmos where quirks ignite.

As we draft in the canvas wide,
A universe where fun can't hide,
For art and chaos go hand in hand,
In every corner of this land.

## Crafting Celestial Whispers

Whispers float on solar winds,
Galactic gnomes pull cosmic strings,
With glue and sparkles, they confide,
In making worlds where giggles hide.

Crafting wishes with lunar dust,
A playground made for playful thrust,
Superstars chuckle, shining bright,
Painting the dark, embracing light.

A telescope peeks with a grin,
Spotting antics of kin and kin,
The sky is full of playful pranks,
In this craft, imagination ranks.

Celestial whispers float and sway,
Creating joy in a cosmic way,
In this laughter-filled expanse,
Where the stars eagerly do their dance.

www.ingramcontent.com/pod-product-compliance
Lightning Source LLC
Chambersburg PA
CBHW071846160426
43209CB00003B/440